Contents

KU-506-946

LiVEWiRE
REAL LIVES

Nelson Mandela

Iris Howden

Published in association with The Basic Skills Agency

Hodder & Stoughton
A MEMBER OF THE HODDER HEADLINE GROUP

Acknowledgements

Photos: p. iv © Camerapress, pp. 6, 17, 19, 21, 23 and 26 © Corbis.
Cover photo: © Popperfoto/Reuter.

Orders: please contact Bookpoint Ltd, 39 Milton Park, Abingdon, Oxon OX14 4TD. Telephone: (44)
01235 400414, Fax: (44) 01235 400454. Lines are open from 9.00–6.00, Monday to Saturday, with a
24 hour message answering service. Email address: orders@bookpoint.co.uk

British Library Cataloguing in Publication Data
A catalogue record for this title is available from The British Library

ISBN 0 340 71156 6

First published 1998
Impression number 10 9 8 7 6 5 4 3 2
Year 2002 2001 2000 1999

Copyright © 1998 Iris Howden

Typeset by Fakenham Photosetting Ltd, Fakenham, Norfolk.
Printed in Great Britain for Hodder & Stoughton Educational, a division of Hodder Headline Plc,
338 Euston Road, London NW1 3BH by Redwood Books, Trowbridge, Wiltshire.

1 A State Visit

In 1996 Nelson Mandela came
on a visit to Britain.
He stayed with the Queen in London.
He rode with her and the Duke
in the royal coach.

Nelson met VIPs at a state banquet.
He made a speech to MPs in the House.
He planted a tree in Hyde Park.

He went on a tour of Brixton, in London.
Thousands came to see him.
Nelson said it was a great honour
– 'for a simple country boy'.

2 A Simple Country Boy

Nelson Mandela was born on 18 July 1918,
in South Africa, just east of Cape Town.
His real first name is Rolihalahla, which means
'pulling the branch of a tree'.
He was given the English name of Nelson
by his teacher when he went to school.

He was the first member of his family
to learn to read and write.
His father was part of the royal family
in a local tribe.
He had four wives.
Nelson's mother was the third.
Nelson had three older sisters.

They lived in round huts in a small village
called Qunu.
His mother grew all the food they needed.
After school Nelson looked after their cows and
goats.
He went out with the other boys to hunt birds.

His father died when Nelson was ten.
He went to live with his cousin. He was a chief.
He paid for Nelson to go to school.
His wife was like a mother to Nelson
and his son, Justice, was like his brother.
Being part of a clan meant
that you looked after your family.

Nelson loved to sit and hear the chiefs
and headmen talk.
They told stories of African kings
and their wars against the British.

Nelson grew up hearing about a time
when South Africa belonged to black people.
When there was no rich or poor.
When all men were equal.
Everyone had a say.
Nelson never forgot this idea.
It stayed with him all his life.

Nelson worked hard and went on to high school.
In his last year, 1940, there was some trouble.
Nelson led a strike of the students.
He would not back down, so he had to leave.

He and Justice ran away to Johannesburg.
They sold two of the chief's cows
to get the train fare.
Their plan was to find work in the mines,
but the chief came to fetch Justice back.
Nelson stayed on to study law.

3 Johannesburg

Johannesburg was known as 'the dark city'.
This was partly because there were no street lights
but also because of the crime.
Gangs ran the city.
Hundreds of men came from the villages
to work in the mines.
They lived in hostels and sent money home.

Nelson lived in a township, which was a slum area.
He worked as a clerk by day and studied at night.
He often walked six miles into town
to save the bus fare so that he could buy candles
to read his books.

Apartheid – a 'whites only' sign in South Africa.

His landlord was very kind.
He gave Nelson a cooked lunch on Sunday.
He also gave him an old suit, which Nelson wore
every day for five years.

It was 1948. There was an election due.
At that time Africans could not vote.
The white people were in control.
There were many laws keeping the races apart.
This was known as 'apartheid'.
It was a system that Nelson knew was wrong.

Black people could not marry whites.
They could not use the same beaches.
Or go the same bars or cafés.
They could not sit on the same seats
in parks or on buses.
They had to carry a pass at all times.

At university Nelson mixed with white students
for the first time.
He met people like Joe Slovo,
who wanted to change the laws.
He met Indians who were also against them.
He got to know Walter Sisulu and Oliver Tambo.
They were to be his friends for life.

4 Marriage

While he was at university,
Nelson met his first wife.
She was Walter's cousin. Her name was Evelyn.
She worked as a nurse to keep the family.
They had their first son, Thembi, in 1945.
Later they had another boy and a girl.

Nelson was a good father.
He helped in the house.
He bathed his children and played with them.
But the marriage did not last.
They split up in 1956. Nelson was spending
too much time away from home.

A year later Nelson met the woman who was to be
his second wife, Winnie Madikizela.
They had two daughters, Zeni and Zindzi.
Winnie, too, was to suffer through Nelson's
struggle to get equal rights for Africans.

In his book, *Long Walk To Freedom*,
Nelson said that the hardest part of that fight
was having to neglect his own family.
He felt guilty that he was not able to care for
his mother or his own children.

5 Politics

In 1953 Nelson set up his own law firm
with Oliver Tambo.
He had reached one goal.
It was not enough.
He could not stand by and see Africans suffer.

Since the mid-1940s he had been a member
of the African National Congress Party (ANC).
The ANC was the party of the African people.
Nelson and his friends in the Youth Wing
took action in Johannesburg with one-day strikes.

One May Day the police fired on the crowd.
Many people died. There was more unrest.

In the 1950s black people's houses were bulldozed.
They were moved out to other areas.
Women were also made to carry passes.

Even children were killed in the violence.

The Government began to change the schools.
Africans were only to be taught to a basic level.
They could not speak their own language in class.
The ANC told students to stay away from school.
Many young blacks like Steve Biko
grew up to be rebels.
The ANC and other groups set out
to break the law.
Hundreds of black Africans and Indians
held protest marches.

Soon mass meetings were banned.
The ANC had to meet in private houses,
talk to people at work, or on the bus.

The party had no money to fund it.
No voice in the media.
They asked for support from other countries.
Nelson got the promise of money and arms.
The ANC saw they were getting nowhere
by peaceful means.
It was time to use force.

A protest march was held in Sharpeville in 1960.
Cars were burned.
Stones were thrown at the police.
The police shot 69 people dead
and wounded 180.
White people began to panic.
They bought guns.

The ANC and the other African party,
the Pan Africanist Congress (PAC),
stepped up the action.
There were more strikes and demonstrations.
Nelson and others burned their passes
in front of a huge crowd.
He was arrested.
Oliver Tambo fled abroad.
He was to live in exile for 30 years.

6 Trials

In 1960 Nelson was put on trial for the first time.
After nine months
the case against him was dropped,
but he was banned from leaving home.
He went into hiding. For months he moved
around in disguise, as a servant or a driver.
He used the name David Motsamai.

In 1962 he was arrested and put on trial again.
In court he wore the leopard skin 'kaross'.
He gave the black salute with his fist
and shouted 'Amandla' – which means freedom.
He was sent to prison for five years.

This was only the beginning.
In 1964 he went on trial again – for treason.
This crime could carry the death penalty.
The Government said the ANC was violent.

Nelson's defence was short.
He said he was guilty of no crime.
The government was to blame for any violence.
For making laws that were unjust.
Nelson was sent back to prison again.
This time his sentence was for life.

7 Prison

Nelson, Walter and others were sent
to Robben Island.
This was the worst prison in South Africa.
The warders were hard men. They carried guns.
Prisoners got up at 5.30. They worked outside
all day, breaking stones, digging lime.

At night they had to wash in cold water,
sleep on thin mats on the floor.
They had no books, no clocks, no news
of the outside world. They could send one letter
and have one visit every six months.

Even in prison, Nelson never gave up.
He stood up for the rights of the prisoners.
He would not eat the bad food
or wear the shorts Africans were given.
Nelson kept his body fit and his mind active.

Through the years he tried to change the system.
He won the right for prisoners to study.
Nelson talked to the warders, trying to make
them see that apartheid was wrong.
He never gave up hope.

Robben Island prison.

8 Free Mandela

In the 1970s, after the shooting of school children
at Soweto, South Africa got a bad press
from the rest of the world.
Nelson Mandela became a symbol for those who
had died.

The USA and France called for his release.
India gave him its highest award.
In Britain, streets were named after him.
Students at London University wanted him as
Chancellor.

Winnie Mandela, who had been given a hard time
by the police, was invited
to speak on his behalf all over the world.

Soon VIPs from other countries began to visit
Nelson in prison. They asked for his release.
President P W Botha was forced
to offer him freedom.
But Nelson stood firm.
He said he was still a member of the ANC
– with the same beliefs.
He would not be free until apartheid was over.

He spent his 70th birthday in prison.
Good wishes poured in from all over the world.

People at a 'Free Nelson Mandela' rally.

It was to be February 1990
before he left prison.
He had spent 27 years locked away.
The crowds were so great
his car could hardly get past.

He spent the first night of freedom
at the home of Bishop Tutu.
Nelson rang Oliver Tambo in Sweden.
Later he flew to Soweto where 120,000 people
turned out at the stadium to greet him.

He carried on talks with the new President
F W de Klerk – the man who helped him
get rid of apartheid.
Later they were to share the Nobel Peace Prize.

Nelson Mandela with Bishop Desmond Tutu.

9 The New South Africa

On 27 April 1994, Nelson's dream came true.
Millions of Africans voted for the first time.
Lines of black people stood for hours
on dusty roads.
Many had waited all their lives for this day.
The ANC took over 60% of the vote.
Nelson Mandela became the country's
first black president.

Nelson was glad that other parties won some seats.
He knew that the only way
to unite South Africa
was for all groups to share the power.

Nelson Mandela votes for the first time.

10 Divorce

One thing spoiled his success.
Stories came out in the press about Winnie.
She had been named in a scandal in Soweto.
Now she and her bodyguards, known as
her 'football team', were put on trial
for the murder of a young boy.

Nelson did not believe that his wife
was guilty of this crime.
But he thought she had been foolish
to get mixed up with these people.

He went to her trial to show his support,
but the couple had grown apart
during his long years in prison.
They no longer saw things in the same way.

At last, in 1992, Nelson told the press
that they were to separate.
He got his divorce from her in 1996.

Later that year he spoke about his new love.
She was Graca Machel, the widow
of the President of Mozambique.

The couple had become close after the death
of her husband in a plane crash.
Graca was willing to share his home
but she said she would not marry Nelson
while he was President of South Africa.

By the mid-1990s Nelson was really only
a 'part-time' president.
He did not want to stand for election again
in April 1999.
He hoped a younger man
would take over the job.

The trouble was that Nelson Mandela was seen
by many as the one person who could
hold together the different groups
that make up South Africa.

There is such a mixture of races.
Even amongst the black people
the tribes cannot agree
on the best way forward.

Nelson Mandela has given his life
to this cause.
It would be fair to allow him happy years.
To enjoy his retirement with the one he loves.